ENTREPRENEUR'S DON'T WORK?

Mark Ryan Puente

TABLE OF CONTENTS

CHAPTER 1

EMPLOYEE

First thing is first whoever said entrepreneurs don't work clearly. has never been an entrepreneur, I work a job that fits my needs pays enough money and allows me to work from home. Some people would even call this a win, but we are not those people we have a bigger picture in mind. *Example: Daymond John started FUBU in 1998 while working at Red Lobster, with only forty dollars in his pocket to invest in his clothing. brand. But while he was working at Red Lobster he was also working on the business between shifts. Later Daymond and his mother even mortgage the house to fund his Dream to generate startup capital. Later in life Daymond quoted, "that was a bad idea", but they took the leap of faith. This brings me to my next point. **IMPORTANT.** When starting in a new business you are going to lose money. But! You are not losing if you do not give up, this is called investing in your dreams. You are going to need to invest in yourself. If you don't know what to do or how to start, then I would recommend finding an already build business that takes some of the risk and in most cases, they are willing to share their business models by teaching you their services and skills or giving you their products with little to no startup cost up front. But remember this, if you are not willing to invest in yourself don't expect anyone else to. Work on yourself work towards your dream work to fund your business.

Notes

ow that you have an idea of why some people become entrepreneurs, what are your reasons?

(Daily Coffee)

There are three types of people in this world: those who make things happen, those who watch things happen, and those who wonder what happened. Which one are you?

CHAPTER 2
MOTIVATION IS TEMPORARY

There are many reasons that people become entrepreneurs, but here are two that I typically find most common, financial difficulties and the dream of becoming your own boss. Whichever your reasons may be this might be enough to get you started but it's not always enough to get you to finish. So, what is? Great question. What are your reasons? What's your why...? Maybe this is a person a child a mother, a father, or a spouse someone who you're emotionally invested in that person who you cannot let down, who is depending on you to succeed. Motivational quotes, videos, etc. I find can be useful resources too. They are like a pick me up, a cup of coffee for your mood when you feel not so encouraged. Eric Thomas, one of my favorite motivational speakers shared a testimony about his mother-in-law's fight with cancer. She was sent home from the hospital they told her the cancer had metastasized inside of her whole body. The doctor said go home and spend some time with your family because there's nothing we can do. People were saying yup that's it for her. But she said that's not it for me. She said "I don't care about what the doctor says I aint done yet, I have two grand kids I need to see graduate and then I might die. but until then I aint done yet. I can get through this, I will get through this, I must get through this!" Fight as if your life depends on it fight for your dreams!

Notes

What's your why? Who is that person? What's that thing that is depending on you to succeed?

(Daily Coffee)

"You will never be successful in life until you want it as bad as you got to breath."

Eric Thomas

CHAPTER 3
OBSESSION BEATS TALENT

One of the greatest examples of obsession I can use in this book is through an athlete who is greatly. admired for his work ethic by peers, Kobe Bryant. Waking up at 4 am to practice before practice Kobe was in love with the sport of basketball. He was so disciplined that he never stops learning since he was a child till his passing. Imagine if you had that level of commitment to your business your marriage or even yourself. Success would look easy to those from the outward looking in, they would say he's just gifted, if I was that tall I would be an amazing basketball player too. But on the contrary Kobe spoke about his flaws and ways to get better. He stated this in an interview "my hands are big but there not massive, I'm quick but not insanely quick, I'm fast but not ridiculously fast. so I have to rely on skills a lot more and angles I had to study the game a

lot more." So now that we know even the best still

work on their flaws to

become better. What do you need to do? What's

holding you back from

reaching a level of success, you could only dream of.

A wealthy man once told me be proud not of your gifts

but of your hard work and your

choices. So even if you're not a pro basketball player

but you might be.

really good at math this is a kind of gift that comes

easy to you. But

practicing that math and taking it to the next level

that could be really.

challenging for you. You can't really be proud of a

gift, you can be.

grateful for them. But you choose to

work hard and choose to do hard things. That's

something to be proud of.

NOTES

Obsessed! You need to wake up, eat, drink, and sleep your passion. What are you doing to ensure your success?

(Daily Coffee)

"In order to achieve the things in life others don't have you must be. Willing to do the things others won't do."

Les Brown

CHAPTER 4
BUILDING AND SETTING GOALS

Being an entrepreneur, we often talk multiple streams of income. In order to become wealthy, you may have heard of the Cash flow. quadrant, the 4 ways to make money. I'll be sure to add this at the end of the book so that I don't get off topic. Now with multiple streams of income in mind we can often get distracted with so much information being thrown at us. Example: if you are in real-estate you shouldn't get into drop shipping by opening up online store, build your brand stay within your niche and then expand! McDonald's is a prime example of this McDonald's doesn't make their money just from selling burgers. Former McDonald's CFO, Harry J. Sonneborn, has quoted, "we are not technically in the food. business. We are in the real estate business. Imagine a milk shake. machine sales associates working with the McDonald brothers, serving as a franchising agent seeing a bigger picture. Franchising is a model by which fast food chains can expand quickly and efficiently by using the money of small investors. Harry perfected new techniques, to increasing the corporation's size while keeping strict control of its products. Around this time is when CFO Sonneborn came up with the McDonald's real estate strategy that the company continues to use today.

So, what does this all mean? They bought the properties and then leased them out at large. markups. In addition to that regular income, the corporation would take a percentage of each shop's gross. sales. Stay hungry my friend and keep building

Notes

It's time to start setting goals start small, weekly goals then monthly next yearly goals.

(Daily Coffee)

"The chains of habit are too light to be felt until they are too heavy to be broken."

Warren Buffet

CHAPTER 5
FAIL YOUR WAY TO SUCCESS

I have worked with so many amazing entrepreneurs and business owners who have dedicated their lives to carrying out their dreams, working all hours of the day to perfecting their craft and never missing an opportunity because that could be the one that will take them to the next level. But I also worked with some that were just waiting on success to happen. Waiting for the perfect time. Breaking news there's no such thing as the perfect time. Remember practice makes progress. The legendary motivational speakers, Les Brown quoted, " you don't have to be great to get started but you have to get started to be great." So, get started. Have a goal in mind set a target. You know the old saying you don't plan to fail but you failed because you didn't plan. You may have the next big idea with no steps to get there. Connect with a mentor find a successful person and ask questions to become a student. Arnold once said, " you could have the most beautiful ship and just drift in circles." Failure is ok just if you don't give up. Failure is the key to success. Don't believe me? Thomas Edison failed 1000 times before successfully creating the light bulb. Need more? Michael Jordan missed more than 9000 shots in his career, he lost almost 300 games. And at least 26 times he was trusted to take the game winning shot and missed. But Michael Jordan neither Thomas Eddison is remembered for their losses only their wins.

Notes

Make a plan and make it plain. Write down what the next five years are going to look like.

(Daily Coffee)

"If you do it in a yard it will be hard but inch by inch
it will be done in a cinch"

Les Brown

CHAPTER 6
PUTTING MONEY TO WORK

So to answer the age old question, do entrepreneurs work? Yes, we work extremely hard every day, because if we stop our money stops. This could be a determining factor for you and ultimately deter people from achieving their dreams. Feeling overwhelmed with the idea of a never-ending race to become wealthy. I know what you're thinking. I don't want to work myself to death with no end. So, what's the solution? Quite simple Making money work for you. Here are some Examples: Through real estate is a great way to have your money to work for you. if you own more than one property you can make what people call passive income, but please don't be fooled this still requires some work. By renting out homes or commercial buildings for people or business. Another example is to write a book. Or investing in people with products by lending startup capital for a business with royalties/percentage, honestly every niche is unique and will require some research that best fits your needs and capabilities plus cash flow. Investors know this all too well no matter if they are investing in stocks, bonds, or even doing some day trading. Need more? Credit card companies are making a large profit from charging you a fee with interest charges don't believe me see how much you really paid for that PS5 or them shoes using that credit card by applying what we know in the financial world as the rule of 72. Just go on YouTube, you're welcome. Which leads to my next point this is extremely important. skills may pay the bills but learning about finances is one of the best investments I could have ever made, you need to learn about your finances. Why? I'm glad you asked. because if someone were to give you a million dollars you better become a millionaire quick, so that you get to keep the money. Let that sink in.

Notes

Put together ideas of how You can make money work for you.

(Daily Coffee)

"You can have more then you want because you can become more then you are"

Jim Rohn

CLOSING STATEMENT

I hope this book was able to inspire something in you or even just give you quick look inside the "job" and or possibilities for you as an entrepreneur. This book does not give you everything you need to be successful I understand that, but it's enough to get you started. look back and if you followed along with the process and filled in the notes then congratulations you just put together your goals, dreams, and a direction of what your future could look like and the reasons behind this new journey. If those things don't line with one another, it's OK, it's better to know so you can make the adjustments. I would like to leave you with one last analogy of a story I once heard of the Chinese bamboo tree. Imagine planting a seed and you watered and nurtured that seed every week, every month, year after year and nothing grew, but you knew you planted that seed, and everyone else around you thought you were crazy because you kept watering that patch of dirt where this seed was planted. But on the fifth year it started to sprout and before you know it that little seed grows to be 90 feet tall after just 6 weeks! Life and business are the same. The big question is did it take 6 weeks or 5 years to grow 90 feet tall? There's no question about it, it took 5 years. Your dream is the seed, you won't see it grow right away but if you stay consistent and in the unseen the dirt the seed is spouting a root big and strong preparing to hold that 90 feet of growth that is ready to take place once it's time. keep watering keep nurturing that dream because your breakthrough is coming it might not be today it might not be tomorrow or even in 3 years from now. But stay consistent don't give up. Become obsessed with your dream and enjoy the process because your success is coming.

The Cash flow Quadrant

In this section you will learn about the four ways to make money.

First: Employee, which this is typically one of the slowest and have the lowest return by trading time for money.

Second: Special skill, like a doctor, lawyer, barber, etc. This enables you to also trade time for money but at a higher price.

Third: business owner, this will allow you to trade other people's time for money.

Lastly: Investor, trading your money for money or other people's money for money.

Notes

Put together some ideas of how You can make money work for you.

(Daily Coffee)

Avoid telling big dreams to a small, minded person.

DAY 1

_____

_____

_____

_____

_____

_____

_____

_____

_____

_____

_____

_____

DAY 2

_____

_____

_____

_____

_____

_____

_____

_____

_____

_____

_____

_____

DAY 3

DAY 4

DAY 5

_____

_____

_____

_____

_____

_____

_____

_____

_____

_____

_____

DAY 6

DAY 7

_____

_____

_____

_____

_____

_____

_____

_____

_____

_____

_____

_____

DAY 8

DAY 9

DAY 10

DAY 11

DAY 12

DAY 13

DAY 14

_____

_____

_____

_____

_____

_____

_____

_____

_____

_____

_____

_____

_____

DAY 15

DAY 16

DAY 17

DAY 18

DAY 19

DAY 20

DAY 21

DAY 22

DAY 23

DAY 24

DAY 25

DAY 26

_____

_____

_____

_____

_____

_____

_____

_____

_____

_____

_____

DAY 27

DAY 28

DAY 29

DAY 30